THE HANDBOOK OF HUMAN OWNERSHIP

A Manual for New Tax Farmers

STEFAN MOLYNEUX

ISBN: 1975654447
ISBN 13: 9781975654443

Contents

THE HANDBOOK OF HUMAN OWNERSHIP
A MANUAL FOR NEW TAX FARMERS

Hey – seriously – congratulations on your new political post!

If you are reading this, it means that you have ascended to the highest levels of government, so it's really, really important that you don't do or say anything stupid, and screw things up for the rest of us.

The first thing to remember is that you are a figurehead, about as relevant to the direction of the state as a hood ornament is to the direction of a car – but you are a very important distraction, the "smiling face" of the fist of power. So hold your nose, kiss the babies, and just think how good you would look on a stamp. A stamp, for mail… No, not email, *mail*. Never mind, we'll explain later.

Now, before we go into your media responsibilities, you must understand the true history of political power, so you don't accidentally act on the naïve idealism you are required to project to the general public.

HUMAN LIVESTOCK – A HISTORY OF TAX FARMING

The reality of political power is very simple: bad farmers own crops and livestock – good farmers own *human beings*.

This is not nearly as simple as it sounds, hence the need for this manual.

1

The very first thing to remember is that you are a *mammal*, an animal, and like all animals, you want to maximize consumption while minimizing effort. By far the most effective way to do this is to take from other people, just as a farmer takes milk and meat from cows.

In the dawn of history, this predation occurred in the most base manner, through brute cannibalism. While this may have proven effective in the short run, it fell prey to the problem of consuming your seed crop, in that it provided only a few meals, whilst re-growing more human livestock took over a decade.

And, it was pretty gross. Sometimes, even after you washed your food, it was too smelly to eat. (Interesting fact: deodorant was first invented as *marinade*.)

The husbandry of human ownership took a giant leap forward with the invention of *slavery*, which was a step up from cannibalism because instead of using people *as* food, it used people to *grow* food, which was a much more sustainable model, to say the least. And far less smelly.

Slavery was an improvement to be sure, but it limited the growth of the ruling class because it could not solve the problem of *motivation*. Turns out, if you treat people like a machine, they end up with the motivation of a machine, which is to break two days after the warranty ends, haha.

Anyhoo, the basic reality of human ownership is this:

1. First, you must first subdue the masses through force
2. Then, you maintain that subjugation through the psychological power of *ethics*.

People think that *ethics* were invented to make people good, but that's like saying that chastity belts were invented to spread STDs. No, no – ethics were invented to bind the *minds* of the slaves, and to create the only true shackles

THE HANDBOOK OF HUMAN OWNERSHIP

we rulers need: guilt, self-attack and a fear of the tyranny of ethics. Whoever teaches ethics rules the herd, because everyone is afraid of bad opinions, mostly from themselves. If you do it right, no judgment will be as evil or endless as the one coming from the mirror.

This is all fairly straightforward – however, the ethics required to control slaves requires the creation of a paradise after death that they can look forward to, if only they continue to obey their masters. This harvests the *muscles* of the slaves, but not their *minds*, which remain depressed and alienated and otherworldly and, well, economically fairly useless. Basically, you're saying "Hey, let's double down, shall we? I'll trade you pretty much everything in this life for everything in the afterlife, mmmkay?" It really only takes a moment's thought to realize that anyone making that deal has no belief in the afterlife - I mean, look at the gold palaces of the Pope, for heaven's sake! - but frankly, a moment's thought appears to be a moment too long for most people.

Tragically, slavery had its limits. Slaves have to be treated as apes that can be verbally commanded, which provides the ruling classes sophisticated control over their *muscles*, but permanently breaks the most valuable resource of the human crop – their *minds*.

The Roman Empire perfected the slave-owning model, but inevitably ended up creating too many dependent slaves, which triggered the slow economic collapse of the entire system. (For more on this, see the section on current conditions below.)

After the Dark Ages, when the ruling classes had to suffer the indignity of retreating into the dank attics of the Church, the feudal model emerged.

The feudal approach improved on the direct slave-owning model by granting the human livestock ("serfs") nominal ownership over land, while taking a portion of their productivity through taxes, military conscription, user fees for grinding grain and so on. So instead of owning folks directly, we just let them sweat themselves into puddles on their little ancestral plots, then took whatever we wanted from the proceeds -- all the while telling them, of course, that God Himself appointed us as masters over them, and that their highest virtue was meek subservience to their anointed masters, blah blah. Again, you might be thinking that, historically, God seems to have had a very soft spot for the most violent, entitled and warlike of His flock – and if meek submission was a virtue, why was it not practiced by the rulers, and so on, but don't worry; you need to just put these entirely natural thoughts right out of your head, because once the people become enslaved, basic reasoning just short-circuits in their tiny minds, so that they do not see the cramped horrors of their little lives.

Anyway, the evolution of medieval serfdom split society into four basic groups:

1. The ruling class (aristocracy);
2. The church (propaganda);
3. The army (enforcement) – and;
4. The serfs (livestock).

The aristocracy – of which you are now a proud member – reaped the rewards; the Church controlled the slaves through ethics; the Army attacked those not subjugated through ethics, and the Serfs paid for the whole show. (The modern equivalents are: the political masters, the media, the police and the taxpayers.)

Since they had partial custodianship of the land, medieval serfs had at least *some* incentive to optimize their agricultural productivity, and so starting from about the 12th century, significant increases in farm production created the excess food required for the development of cities, the natural home of the ruling classes.

The economic development of cities remained dependent upon the rediscovered Roman law, which was not a free market/private property legal system, and so economic productivity remained relatively stagnant, at least compared to the 18th century to the present.

Medieval guilds were ridiculously inefficient, forcing father-to-son transmission of livelihoods, requiring ridiculously lengthy apprenticeships designed to raise barriers to entry, denying advertising and marketing opportunities, and so on.

Furthermore, the Catholic Church had banned usury, or the lending of money for interest, which prevented investment in economic improvements. (This was largely due to the fact that the Church, and the Aristocracy it served, did not want to pay interest on its debts.)

(All of these early economic inefficiencies hindered the development of democracy, which requires enormous reserves of capital, used as collateral to bribe voters in the present with the money of the future.)

The splintering of Christendom into warring factions during the Reformation created new opportunities for capital accumulation and loans, and the economic warfare that resulted was really a conflict between medieval capital inefficiencies and the new investment efficiencies available under Protestantism – and Judaism to some degree. Naturally, the religion that was able to borrow the most won, and lending money for interest became an established practice throughout society, thus paving the way for the Industrial Revolution.

Also, after hundreds of years of bloody religious warfare where priests were effectively trying to gain control of the military might of the state, in order to impose their doctrines on everyone else, the separation of church and state became a matter of base survival. Prying religious doctrines away from government policies meant that some vaguely rational approaches to property rights and trade could be achieved, which gave rise to arguments for free trade, notably by Ricardo and Adam Smith.

When you stop trading in God, you can start trading in goods.

Starting in the 17th century, the agricultural productivity that the cities depended on began to falter. Serf landholdings were willed to sons, which created increasing fragmentation of properties, and inevitable inefficiencies in sowing and plowing. The ruling classes, eager to remain in the cities rather than go back to the damp and dirty countryside, forced the enclosure movement on the peasants, consolidating landholdings and driving hundreds of thousands of serfs off their ancestral lands. This almost immediately increased agricultural productivity, saving the cities – while creating a massive army of cheap labor which, having no land to farm anymore, inevitably ended up looking for work in towns.

The conditions were thus ripe for the Industrial Revolution – capital freedom, a mass of cheap labor, some free trade, excess food, and the growing religious skepticism which resulted from the wonderful advances of the scientific method, followed since the 16th century.

It was at some point during this period that the greatest leap forward in human ownership came to pass, which was *the simple genius of allowing the livestock to choose their own occupations.*

At one fell swoop, the problem of livestock motivation was largely solved – at least until the present. Rather than eat the human livestock, or own them directly, or force them into specific occupations, a free market was created for the *source* of wealth, while the enslavement aspect was shifted to the *effects* of wealth, i.e. wages and capital.

Labor was free, wages were taxed – this was the greatest leap forward in human farming history! All prior ruling classes were revealed as incompetent parasites, compared to the brilliant manipulations of the modern human harvester!

The economic predations of the ruling classes still remained, but became largely invisible. Tariffs and duties were buried in the prices paid by consumers, who had no comparison prices to see their effects. The softening of the visible whip to a kind of leeching fog gave the livestock the *perception* of freedom – and they all stampeded to work, to wealth, and to fatten our tables in a way we had never dreamed possible!

The trapped entrepreneurial energies of the human herd were thus unleashed for the first time in history, producing a staggering superabundance of wealth and products and services, portions of which were hoovered up to the ruling classes to a degree never before experienced!

The benefits were clear, the productivity increases astounding – but the complications of managing this semi-free horde of human livestock rose exponentially as well.

The first and greatest danger was the shift from *aristocracy* to *meritocracy*, or the reality that greater wealth could be accumulated through trade and creativity rather than tax pillaging and the control of state violence. (This was same danger faced by the Church in the shift from superstition to science.)

The rising entrepreneurial class created an uncomfortable split within society, in which the benefits of the aristocracy began to be openly questioned. Societies like America were founded without any aristocracy at all – and aristocracies across Europe faced mounting rebellions, and sometimes outright extinction.

The aristocracy did not want to crush the entrepreneurial class – since it was so wonderfully productive – but it could not allow itself to be eclipsed by these entrepreneurs, and so another unnamed genius came up with a delightfully playful solution called *incorporation*.

The entrepreneurial classes wanted to maximize their profits, of course, and sometimes this came at the expense of the workers. In the early 19th century, citizens had access to a common law legal system that allowed them to bring suit against their employers for death, mutilation, pollution and so on. The capitalists wanted to avoid these legal attacks of course, but no one wanted to explicitly strip the workers of these rights, otherwise they would become aware of their enslavement, and would lose their motivation, and we would be right back to the Middle Ages again, which no one wanted at all!

Across the Western world, government after government introduced the concept of *incorporation*, a brilliant stroke in the annals of human ownership! Incorporation created a legal fiction called a *corporation* which shielded entrepreneurs, capitalists, managers and owners from most legal repercussions for their misdeeds – and even losses within their businesses!

Entrepreneurs could now take money out of this "corporation" and keep it for themselves, while if any legal action succeeded against them, or their businesses lost money or went into debt, it was now the "corporation" and "shareholders" and employees that paid the price, and no one could ever come after their personal assets. It was like a casino where you kept your winnings, and strangers paid your losses.

In return for extending this legal shield to the capitalists, our political class took a cut in the form of corporate taxes – most of which came from dividends and wages of course. This effectively trapped the entrepreneurs in the service of the state, ensuring that they would *never* seek to eclipse or make redundant the political class, since they were now dependent upon State power for the maintenance of their legal shield and one-way economic privileges.

THE 19TH CENTURY

The 19th Century was a wildly creative time in the history of human livestock ownership. The amazing productivity unleashed by the privatization of labor, and the partial socialization of wages, created such prosperity that the necessity of the ruling classes itself was called into question.

Furthermore, the increased education and economic initiatives of the working classes threatened the economic value of the managerial classes. The workers achieved almost complete literacy, and possessed excellent work ethics, legal knowledge and social networks, including the so-called Friendly Societies, which shielded the poor from destitution through any of life's many accidents.

The supply of those able to *manage* thus increased, which drove down the price of management – which was not exactly welcomed by the existing capitalists.

The traditional solution to increased competition from the poor was to ban books and education, inflict religious guilt about materialism, or start a war – none of which were politically or economically advantageous at the time. Openly banning education for the children of the poor would have reintroduced the "OMG I'm a total slave!" demotivation problem; religious belief was waning, while war would have destroyed all the new capital that the ruling and entrepreneurial classes were enjoying.

In a brilliant stroke, the ruling classes and the Church conspired to create a false educational "emergency." In conjunction with a large number of resentful and underperforming teachers, public school education was introduced with the stated goal of improving the skills, abilities and intelligence of the poor.

Naturally, the true goal was the exact opposite. Rather than focusing on practical, economic and entrepreneurial knowledge, government schools quickly shifted the educational focus towards patriotic history, rote memorization and recitation, Latin and Greek, and an endless plethora of other useless and boring trivia. This was the sports equivalent of forcing your competition to take naps instead of training, resulting in a truly delightful absence of competition for medals. Government schools created dull, resentful drones only fit for taking orders, so the threat to the managerial class was averted. (All this started in Prussia, which was medieval, mystical and militaristic, which should have been something of a clue for everyone, but again, thought hurts, apparently.)

One of the four pillars of the human farm, the Church, faced mounting challenges in the 19th century, as the increased secularism of the Industrial Revolution and the growth in the empirical value of the scientific method undermined the superstitious terrors of the Middle Ages.

Sensing that the power of their God was on the decline, the clergy began casting about for a new home. Their expertise was in sophistic ethics, remember, rather than political power, and so they came up with a wonderful idea that allowed them to bring their brilliant historical lies into politics, but without having to enter into the sordid knuckle fights of base democratic electioneering.

In a word: *socialism*.

Socialism, or communism as it is sometimes called, is merely a secular religion, where the State becomes a god. It has its good and evil, its creation myths, its eventual heaven where the State withers away, its ruling class of ethical liars, and so on. Priest as Plato, you get the picture…

Suddenly, instead of heaven existing in the afterlife, it was promised in this life, as soon as government programs succeeded. (The afterlife is far more likely!) The new Socialist clergy promised an end to poverty, injustice, illiteracy, shortness, baldness – any word they could get their grubby hands on - and of course anyone who disagreed with these fantasies was immediately portrayed as pro poverty, injustice, illiteracy etc. Of course, just as the moral guilt of religion can never create virtue, government programs can never create paradise, and so a perpetual motion machine of social control was started, where the supposed "solutions" just created more of the same problems.

Religion and Kiddies

Religion has always been used to support and extend the power of the State, through a number of powerful psychological mechanisms, always inflicted on children.

First of all, in religion, success is guilt, and failure is legitimate need. Creating guilt among economically successful people plants a seed that flowers into a guilty parting with their property for the sake of "helping the poor." (Notably, priests never seem to get round to attacking their own successful head priests, or the successful political systems they support and enrich.)

Secondly, religion excels at creating nonexistent entities, and then promoting a class of specialized liars who claim to speak for those entities. Thus you have a "god," and a priest who speaks "for that god." In socialism, you have the poor, and you have those who speak "for the poor." (Notably, it doesn't really matter that socialists almost never come from "the poor," such as Marx and Engels, two unemployed rich kids who claimed to have earthshaking insights into the poverty-stricken working classes, who were actually getting richer.)

Thirdly priests, like politicians, promote arbitrary but universal ethics, while excluding themselves from the moral rules they impose, which is the most fundamental attribute of any ruling class, as we will see below.

Fourthly religion – again, like the State – promotes wonderful traps in the form of false dichotomies. For example, if you don't want to the State to steal your income in order to "help the poor," then according to religion you must hate the poor. This is like saying that if you object to getting raped, you must hate lovemaking.

We could go on with this, but since religion has been so thoroughly absorbed into the State in the form of socialism, there's little point in examining its medieval corpse.

THE MODERN WORLD

In the past, society was so poor that the aristocracy had to be hereditary in order to maintain its economic wealth – this is no longer the case, due to the massive productivity increases of the relatively free market. Now, a successful politician can easily gather enough wealth to last several generations – or forever if handled wisely – in just a few terms. This has allowed for the development of the illusion that the tax livestock control something we call "democracy."

Because we can steal so much wealth in such a short amount of time, the ruling classes have agreed to rotate in and out of power, in order to maintain the illusion that there is no ruling class. This rotation is essential to maintaining the optimism of the livestock by giving them the belief – almost always false – that they too can join the ruling class. This means that the ruling class is no longer directly exclusive, but rather somewhat permeable, at least at the fringes.

(The modern democratic system has the advantage of transferring literally trillions of dollars from the workers to the rulers – a plunder unprecedented in human history – but the logic of our system is inherently self-destructive, which is why it is important for you, as a new political leader, to make sure that you extract as much money as possible before the whole house of cards comes crashing down. We will tell you how to do this later.)

The democratic system only really came into its own with the abandonment of the gold standard, and the introduction of merely paper currency. Governments in the 19th century – and before – were limited in the amount they could bribe supporters and dependents by the amount of gold they had in their vaults. Gold cannot be created by printing presses, and so abandoning the gold standard (the capacity for citizens to redeem paper money for gold) allowed the printing presses of government bribery to work overtime, creating a good deal of the so-called "wealth" of the post Second World War period.

Democratic governments – like all governments – are all about the forced transfer of wealth from the productive to the unproductive. When the creation of money was limited by actual gold, it was more or less a zero-sum game. When you stole from one group to give to another – always taking your cut – it was a direct reduction and increase of wealth in the present, which was not only highly evident, but also gave the group being stolen from a good deal of incentive to fight the theft.

With the introduction of fiat currency, this all changed. The unimaginative ascribed this to the advent of Keynesianism, but the truth is that fiat currencies predated Keynesianism, and Keynesianism was merely the intellectual cover for the greatest intergenerational theft in history.

When governments can print their own money, politicians can sell future generations off to bribe supporters in the present – and shaft the poor at the same time! If the government adds 5% to the currency in circulation, those closest to the government get to spend that money first – at the prior valuation, before inflation hits – and then, as the additional money spreads through the economy, the price of everything rises, since you have more money relative to goods than you had before, and those at the bottom and the outskirts of the economy – generally the poor, and those on fixed incomes – get hit the hardest.

Thus printing money serves two major purposes – first, it gives free cash to politicians to bribe their supporters; second, it creates and exacerbates poverty on the outskirts of the economy, thus giving an excuse for politicians to raise taxes, create more government programs (and thus more supporters and dependents) and print more money, thus closing the circle.

Fiat currency also allows for luxurious indulgences in social engineering – you can create "wars" on everything (since war is the health of the State, just as the State is the health of war) – drugs, poverty, prostitution, gambling, illiteracy, sickness – whatever. This creates more and more people dependent on State payouts, and scares everyone through terrifying attacks on ordinary human vices. It also changes the kinds of people who want to become enforcers – sorry, "cops" – but again, more on that later.

Unfortunately, the relationship between increases in the money supply and inflation has been too well established and understood to be of much use anymore. Capital markets are always on the lookout for the overprinting of money, and punish governments by increasing the price of their bonds, or downgrading their credit ratings. This is just another reason why we are approaching the end of the current cycle of human ownership.

The second trick that governments can use to bribe those around them is to refrain from pumping money directly into the economy, but rather to create imaginary money, and use it to buy their own government bonds. All this does is push the liability of the repayment of bonds – both interest and principal – into the future. It is a mere accounting trick, like just about everything else the government does, but fools more than enough people to keep the game going just a little bit longer.

Democracy and Bribery – But I Repeat Myself...

Every politician must promise, say, three dollars in benefits for every dollar taken in taxes. This is utterly impossible, of course, since the government has no money of its own, and is ridiculously inefficient at everything it tries – so it is only through borrowing or printing money that politicians are able to bribe voters into imagining that the government produces wealth. The introduction of fiat currency, and the modern banking system, protected by government-controlled cartels – as well as the legal shield called the "corporation" – has been a godsend to modern politicians, since it allows the costs of present day bribery to be pushed off decades or even generations into the future. This has been a complete no-brainer for everyone involved – free bribe money, paid for by strangers who haven't even been born yet, is a temptation too lucrative and consequence-free to even *imagine* resisting.

Technically, democracy is a money-drug addiction that wages war on drugs far less addictive and destructive.

THIS IS THE END...

Unfortunately - and you will see this as an inevitable pattern of the ruling classes' use of violence – this unsustainable system is nearing the end of its current cycle.

The problem is that the consequences of these inevitable national debts are producing medieval conditions once again. First of all, the economic engine of the productive classes – access to capital – is failing, because governments are stealing all the capital in order to bribe voters. It's true that voters then often buy stuff, but that's not quite the same as driving new entrepreneurial development, since voters don't invest in new businesses, but rather buy products from existing businesses – which is yet another reason why existing businesses are big fans of the government!

Secondly, and perhaps more importantly, the issue of livestock de-motivation is raising its ugly head once more. Young people now instinctively grasp the economic catastrophes ahead, and this blunts their ambition and creativity to the point where fewer and fewer new entrepreneurs are creating wealth for the ruling classes.

BIRTHRATES

To rulers, the most fundamental capital is not money, but *people* (or, more accurately, *children*, but we will get to that below.)

Reasonably intelligent human beings do not breed well in captivity, which is why the birthrates of modern Western nations have crashed so catastrophically. Those of us in the ruling class obviously want human livestock intelligent enough to create wealth for us – but unfortunately that kind of intelligence is also easily high enough to do a rational calculation on the benefits and costs of modern parenthood.

In the current system, most parents have to work outside the home in order to sustain even a middle-class existence, because of enormously high taxation, regulation, inflation, debt and economic controls. So parents don't get to spend days with their children, but instead get them for the evenings, night times and mornings, which are in general the least enjoyable times for parenting, particularly when you have to rush kids out of the house to daycare or school. Parents work a full day, get stuck on the terrible roads we built for them, stressed out because they don't want to be late picking up their kids, then bring their kids home, and cook and feed and bathe them, and then try and get them to bed – with precious little playtime. Mom and dad then fall into an exhausted, sexless bed, praying that their children don't wake up at night – and then have to rouse them at an artificial time, get them fed and clothed and out the door on a strict schedule – all of which is anathema to children – and then pay a significant amount of their after-tax income for strangers to take care of the children they so rarely see!

It doesn't take a genius to realize that this is a pretty raw deal for parents, and this is the most fundamental reason why birthrates among our tax cattle are so low – except among the poor, who we pay to breed, so that we can use them to guilt the better-off into surrendering their money to us.

Thus we have de-motivated young people, who spend forever draining wealth – their own and others' – in school and university; fewer babies and children, and a massive bulge of baby boomers heading into retirement, where a completely empty cupboard awaits them.

Citizens can easily understand how impossible this all is, but they shy away from confronting it, or demanding that we change it – or even admitting it – because they're all so guilty at having accepted bribes their whole life, and because parents so rarely want to admit to their kids that they have royally screwed them out of a future, and sold them off to strangers for cut-rate park admissions. These aging citizens need the next generation to pay for their own retirement, but are leaving them with a cratered economy, growing state power and massive national debts, and so to admit guilt would mean – at any reasonable moral level – withdrawing their demands for retirement funding. If a man steals a woman's car, any real apology requires that he give it back – but this is never going to happen with the national debt, or the trillions in unfunded liabilities, and so no one with any real influence is ever going to demand that we deal with this impossible situation.

Democracy is all about the guilty and shameful pillaging of the helpless and unborn; it corrupts moral responsibility to the point where almost everyone is far too guilty and entitled to take a moral stand for accountability.

Get a man to take stolen goods, and he will never complain about theft. This is the essence of democracy.

So – no worries there.

THE DEPENDENT CLASSES

A key foundation of livestock management is *bribery*, which has an obvious benefit – and a subtle one. The obvious benefit is that, say, artists and intellectuals who receive government money will never be fundamentally critical of government taxes and redistribution, for reasons too obvious to mention here. The more subtle benefit is that when you create an entire class of people dependent on government handouts, you divide the livestock into warring factions. Those whose money is being stolen have a strong incentive to reduce State theft, while those who receive stolen money have a strong incentive to increase State theft.

It is absolutely, absolutely essential that you create and maintain conditions which foster slave on slave aggression. If rulers smack down the slaves directly, the livestock immediately become aware of their enslavement, which reintroduces the motivation problem. Efficient human masters thus ensure that the slaves attack each other – the benefits of this are almost too numerous to count, but a few will be mentioned below.

Human beings, as interdependent tribal mammals, have evolved to be terrified of horizontal social attack, ostracism and rejection. This is a core emotional vulnerability which can never be eliminated, and will always serve you well.

Prehistoric man could not live without the support of the tribe, and so the need for social acceptance was programmed into the very base of his brain, as a core survival mechanism. The philosophers who serve power – mostly priests and academics – have layered onto this basic mechanism the additional power of ethics.

Ethics is a claim to a universal principle of preferred behavior, which has the enormous benefit of being easily internalized by the slave classes. If you can get slaves to attack themselves for daring to question the existing social structure, you will not have to lift a finger to keep them in their chains – they will in fact attack anyone holding a key!

As a backup, you must always have a group of slaves willing to attack anyone who mentally frees himself from your false ethics. This enforcement will always come from two main areas: the family and the media.

THE SLAVE FAMILY

Deep down, slaves always know that they're slaves, and their only real enslavement is resisting this knowledge. Prior ruling classes did not trust this basic mechanism, and so were hesitant to substitute horizontal social control for vertical political violence.

Now, we know better.

All commonly accepted cultural myths are created by the ruling class, are essential lubricants for the wheels of power.

The most common cultural myth is that your family is everything, the most important relationship, the most essential intimacy, the most fundamental social unit.

This helps the ruling class in countless ways — not least of which is that it establishes and extends the principle that an accident of birth creates a fundamental and eternal moral obligation; "family" thus equals "country." (Also: "sports team," which is one reason why we fund them.)

Once you have enslaved one generation, most parents will almost inevitably resist the freedom of the next generation, out of guilt and shame about their own surrender.

We tell people to stay close to their families, because their families will so often attack them for even thinking about leaving the cages of collective history.

Let's look at the sequence.

A man surrenders his liberty for petty cash and the illusion of security. He then becomes a father. His son questions his father's moral courage and integrity, and the father then attacks the son, chaining them in a cage they both rot in.

For this cycle to be maintained, we must forever tell the son that his family is the most important thing in the world – more important than reason, evidence, truth, integrity, morality – you name it! If he believes us, and if his family is not committed to his freedom, we (and they) will own him forever.

This is the basic deal we offer to parents, just like priests: *give us your kids, and we'll teach them to honor and obey you no matter what, so you don't actually have to be a good person and earn their respect.*

(True, not all parents take this unholy deal, but we just get the media to mock the homeschooled kids and all is well.)

Furthermore, given the billions of people ensnared in the dependent classes the world over, it is a near-certainty that at least one or more close family members will be dependent upon the existing system, and will then violently attack anyone who questions the morality and practicality of predatory democracy. Want to privatize education? Say hi to your teacher Aunt Mamie, and let the fun begin!

The Media

A few people, however, will retain the strength to emerge from the slave class, and – particularly given the communications opportunities of the Internet – may start broadcasting their message to a wider audience – in which case, it's important to pull the emergency backup attack switch called the "mainstream media."

How do you create slave on slave violence through the mainstream media?

Again, subtlety and trust in the inevitability of human psychology is the key.

First of all, you must never directly censor and control the media, or its inhabitants may rebel against your authority, and reveal your naked aggression. Once the knowledge of slavery becomes inescapable, society inevitably and immediately changes – and hiding this knowledge is the entire art and science of human ownership.

Thus you need to create a slow and increasing economic dependence in the media, rather than arresting and imprisoning its members.

You do this by making reporters more and more dependent upon information from the government. It is much, much cheaper to simply rewrite a governmental press release than it is to spend weeks or months going undercover, interviewing subjects, verifying sources, and exposing yourself to legal complications in order to break a story outside the normal channels of communication.

Furthermore, as State power grows, more and more people become more and more interested in what the government says and does, since they are investors or business people whose fortunes rise and fall on the whims of the ruling class.

This process can be a little risky at first, but you only need a decade or two in order for it to become almost universal and irreversible.

Remember – it takes a pretty empty person to rewrite government press releases for a living, and fairly delusionary managers to pretend that they are not the mere amplifiers of the whispers of power. Once these managers assume their positions, they will inevitably reject any energetic truth seekers, and instinctively seek out and employ other empty rewriters of State edicts. The collective delusion that they're still producing "news" becomes progressively stronger, to the point where they will rail against and attack anyone who actually tries to publish something that is true, particularly if it threatens the government contacts who supply their disinformation.

Access to government thus becomes the foundation of any media organization – therefore no fundamental criticisms of government can be produced. You can criticize a tax, but not taxation itself. You can criticize a party, but not the State. You can criticize a vote, but not voting.

As usual, it is both depressing and exciting to see the tiny price that people are willing to sell themselves for – their name in print, a meager expense account, a few parties, and they are yours.

The physical abuse required to keep the sheep in line is doled out by the police – the verbal abuse is doled out by the media.

The media has been trained to attack anyone who questions the foundations of violent power. The equation is really very simple – so simple that it is always overlooked. If a man says that coercive wealth transfers – *theft*, in the vernacular – are wrong, then the media instantly attacks him for not caring about whoever is receiving the stolen money.

For instance, if a man questions the morality and practicality of the welfare state, he will be immediately attacked for not caring about the poor. If he argues against government schools, then he *clearly* hates the fact that children get educated. If he defends free-trade, he is an immoral advocate for bloodsucking corporations; if he criticizes military budgets, he is a cowardly appeaser who wishes to surrender Fort Knox to Al Qaeda; if he holds people morally accountable for their actions, he is punishing them for their past mistakes and "playing the blame game"; if he refuses to forgive unrepentant wrongdoers, he is nursing a grudge and so on.

If he argues that adult relationships are voluntary, then he is viciously anti-community; if he says that abuse should not be tolerated in relationships, then he is an intolerant absolutist bent on destroying all relationships…

This list can go on and on and on – and Lord knows it does, every day – but you get the point.

The wonderful thing is that you won't ever have to tell the media to do this – it just happens of its own accord, because people who are expert verbal abusers always rise to the top of the media pyramid, because they are so useful to those of us in power, so we always give them access and exclusivity.

You only need a few verbal abusers in charge, and everyone else will fall in line, because anyone who tries to stand up against them will be immediately smacked down, and will face the horrifying spectacle of watching all of their colleagues either take cowardly steps back, or joining in the verbal assaults.

(I should probably have mentioned that priests – the best verbal abusers in history – left the church for socialism *and* the media, which is why the media tends to be so left-wing.)

The reason the media performs this service for us is very simple – we own their livelihoods through licensing, legal regulation and access to information. If we decide to cut anyone off, his career is over. If anyone displeases us, we can threaten to pull the license of the entire organization, because the rules are so Byzantine that we can nail someone for something at any time – much like tax code, it is a form of soft totalitarianism that we have perfected over the generations.

The purpose of regulation is to control through rational anxiety rather than dictatorial terror. Prior dictatorships would shoot people, arrest and imprison them arbitrarily – this controlled people's bodies very effectively, but destroyed their entrepreneurial energies and motivations.

It is far more effective to regulate and license and tax – and this is true for all industries – because potential dissidents then face their own foggy walls of vague anxiety – in which they will not face arrest and imprisonment, but rather lengthy legal complications, which they may eventually win, but which drain much of the joy out of living while they go on, month after month, year after year.

This is true for public-sector unions as well – we don't make it *illegal* for a manager to fire a unionized employee, because that would expose the system for the economic joke that it is – we just make it really, really lengthy and complicated and emotionally draining and confrontational and exhausting – that is the true perfection of soft totalitarianism. People will surrender to anxiety and still vaguely feel free – if you terrorize them directly, they tend to just collapse intellectually and emotionally.

If the media were directly owned by the government, the propaganda would be clear; the indirect "ownership" of licensing and access to information is far more effective and powerful, because it maintains the veneer of independence and critical thinking.

This form of indirect ownership is the essence of modern democratic tax farming.

It is a central truism of human nature that people always attack what they avoid – if a reporter imagines that he is some sort of freethinking iconoclast, he is in complete denial about the reality of his enslavement. This denial always manifests itself in hysterical attacks against anyone who dares to point it out, or who is actually a freethinker.

To sum up – if we attack the slaves, we lose – if the slaves attack each other, which is so easy to orchestrate – we win, at least for a time.

CHILDREN: THE GREATEST RESOURCE

When we say that human beings are the greatest resource, it's important to be precise about what we mean.

Human beings are naturally born with two characteristics – the first is a resistance to arbitrary authority, and the second is a natural susceptibility to obeying universal ethics.

Anyone who doubts the first characteristic has never tried to parent a two-year-old, and anyone who doubts the second has never triggered or experienced moral guilt.

Domesticating the human animal does not mean that everyone needs to turn out the same – in fact, it would be quite a disaster for us if they did.

To most efficiently control the human farm, you need a majority of broken, self-attacking, insecure, shallow, vain and ambitious sheep, forever consumed by inconsequentialities like weight, abs and celebrities – and a minority of volatile, angry and dominant sheepdogs, which you can dress up in either a green or a blue costume, and use to threaten and manage the herd.

Ruling classes have always had to separate children from their parents, otherwise it is almost impossible to substitute weird abstractions like "the state" or "a god" for the parent-child bond. Human children, like ducklings, will bond with whatever person or institution raises them, which is why we always need to get children – hopefully as young as possible – to bond with the State through government daycare and… "education" I guess is the closest word.

In the distant past, rulers made the error of forcibly removing children from their parents, which exposed their enslavement, and so destroyed their motivation. In the late Middle Ages, children were farmed out to wet-nurses, destroying the parent-child bond. In more recent times, the boarding school system separated children from their parents, destroying empathy and creating wonderfully brutal administrators and enforcers for a variety of European empires. (See: *George Orwell.*)

In our constant quest to perfect human ownership, we have found a far better way to break these family bonds, and substitute allegiance to ourselves, in the form of patriotism and/or religiosity.

It's one of those beautiful win-win situations that come along so rarely – first, we raised taxes to the point where it became very difficult to maintain a reasonable lifestyle if one parent stayed home with the children. We also funded feminist groups to the tune of billions of dollars – one of the greatest investments we ever made – to encourage women to abandon their children and enter the workforce.

Not only did this help break the parent-child bond, but it also moved women's labor from nontaxable to taxable – a delightful coincidence of self-interest and practicality for us!

With both parents working, all we had to do was create a few scares about the quality of child care, allowing us to move in to control and regulate that industry, remaking it to serve us best.

In some countries, like the United States, children are effectively removed from parental care by the state within a few weeks or months after birth – in other countries, parents receive direct subsidies to stay at home, which is quite funny when you think about it (and there is precious little room for humor in much of this). We take money by force from the parents, keep a large portion for ourselves, use another portion to run up debts that their children will somehow have to pay off – and then dribble a few pennies down to the mother, who then feels that we are somehow doing her a great favor by allowing her to stay at home!

It is a delicious irony that everyone remains so totally blind to reality that they run to us to protect their children from all kinds of harm, while we are the ones selling off their children's future through national debts! It really is like hiring a thief to guard your property, and the amazing thing is that this is all so completely obvious, and never, ever spoken about!

Sometimes, it would be tempting to feel bad about ruling people, but really, they are so very stupid that it seems almost helpful.

Parenting has generally improved over the centuries, which also poses a grave threat to us, because if children are raised without aggression, they will both immediately see, and never accept, the reality of human ownership.

As parenting has improved, it has become more important for us to intervene earlier and earlier. In the 19th century, it was okay to wait until the tax kittens were five or six before we started propagandizing them in government schools. However, as parenting has improved – particularly in the post-Second World War period, we have had to start intervening earlier and earlier, which is why we try and get at kids so soon after birth now.

When kids were raised fairly well in the post-war period, it produced the disasters of the rebellious 1960s, which almost finished us, and so we began funding radical feminism, controlling teachers more and snatching the kids earlier and earlier to fix all that.

So – we need some parents to create the sheep, and other parents to create the wolves, or the sociopaths who can be relied upon to attack whoever we point to. These sociopaths can be divided into those who guard the ruling class (the police and soldiers and prison guards and so on) – and the criminals that we always wave around to frighten people into running back to our "protection."

Again, the amount of doublethink required to maintain the delusion that the ruling class is not invested in crime – when even by our rules, we are all criminals – is really quite astounding! Governments control almost the entire environment of the poor, from public housing to food stamps to welfare checks to public schools – and it is this environment that produces the majority of criminals! For instance, governments require that children spend about 15,000 hours being educated in state schools, and yet when they emerge from this massive investment as illiterate and violent criminals, no one *ever* takes us to task!

Never, ever underestimate the degree to which people will scatter themselves into a deep fog in order to avoid seeing the basic realities of their own cages.

The strongest lock on the prison is always avoidance, not force.

NEVER-NEVER LAND

Imagine a world in which almost all children were raised peacefully – there would be no criminals, no police, no soldiers, no politicians (or others with a bottomless lust for power) – no bullying in the workplace, no white-collar predations on the general wealth, no assault, no rape, no murder, no theft, no drug abuse, no smoking, no alcoholism, no eating disorders, no pedophilia, far fewer mental and physical health issues, very little divorce, promiscuity or infidelity – since all of these dysfunctions can be directly traced back to early childhood traumas.

What need would such a world have for rulers?

That is the world we can never allow to come into existence.

Anything we can do to traumatize children serves the hierarchical violence of our power.

Getting kids into daycare is a great start, since daycare makes children continually ill, exposes them to the wild aggressions of dozens of other children, destroys the one-on-one time that children need for bonding and emotional maturity. Daycare kids remain insecure, unbonded with a consistent caregiver (since teacher turnover is so high), and end up inevitably placing more emphasis on peer relationships than they do on adult caregiver relationships – including their parents.

These peer relationships among kids inevitably devolve to the lowest common denominator, with bullies and manipulators and the physically attractive rising to the top, and the sensitive and intelligent and empathetic hiding under tables. Children quickly perceive that adult attention is almost always negative – in other words that they *themselves* are negative – serving only to increase the stress of their caregivers. Due to the shortage of time and resources, conflicts between children are rarely resolved in a just manner, but merely with separation and mutual punishment, which breaks the child's natural desire for integrity and virtue, and places all the power in the fists of those empty and dangerous children who do not fear retribution.

When the stressed-out parent comes to pick up the child from daycare, the child feels further devalued, knowing that he is just another source of aggravation for his parent ("Just get in the car!"). The practical necessities of child raising are then compressed into a very short and taxing time, which no one really enjoys. Parents are short-tempered and impatient, children are stressed and unhappy, and then the whole thing starts all over again when the alarm bells go off the next morning.

Children have to feel herded and controlled by impatient adult caregivers long before we get a hold of them in schools, otherwise our whole system will fall apart.

Children have to feel that they are inconvenient impositions on all-powerful authorities long before they become adults – or even schoolchildren – otherwise we will have no control over them.

Children have to feel grateful for whatever crumbs of attention and consideration fall their way, and learn to live on very little, otherwise they will never grow up with the desperate hunger that can only be filled by conformity, patriotism, sports addictions, religions and other superstitions.

We plant children; we grow power.

Rule by Adjective

The violence of the government can create nothing, so all we can do is manipulate language. This is called the "rule by adjective," or RBA.

RBA essentially consists of the creation of noble sounding phrases that completely disintegrate under the slightest rational or empirical examination. The goal is to use wording that sounds like the tagline of a B-grade action movie, but with flags.

A few examples we are particularly proud of:

- "Building a bridge to the 21st century."
- "[Insert country here] has a date with destiny."
- "No dream is beyond our reach."
- "We're one people bound together by a common set of ideas."
- "Let's celebrate our diversity."

In crafting political language, it's essential to play upon personal relationships, and pretend that the farmers and the sheep are all one big happy family, and that anyone who expresses skepticism or disagreements is not a "team player," and does not want to achieve anything noble or great or good or unselfish. For example:

- "There may be naysayers among us who say that we cannot achieve these great things together, but I say that history will prove them wrong, that the spirit of creativity and unity still lives within our people, and that the final chapter of our civilization has yet to be written!" etc etc.

Notice that no substantial criticism is ever addressed – rather, sly slander is continually layered over the objection until whoever objects is just kind of disliked. (This trick is continually reinforced in movies, where all the bad guys are unlikable, and all the good guys likable, which as anyone who has ever read Socrates knows, is almost always the complete opposite of the truth.)

Now that you have achieved the summit of political power, it is also essential that you project calm, confidence, serenity, and all the other characteristics that are completely inappropriate to the imminent disasters awaiting the tax cattle.

The way that you do this is very easy – know that you will now be taken care of for the rest of your life, and your children will never have to work, and their children will never have to work, and you will never face any significant legal problems or disciplinary action or face arrest for anything you have done, even if it means starting unjust wars, murdering people by the hundreds of thousands, imprisoning non-criminals by the millions, running up trillions in debt, authorizing torture, you name it, it's OK.

Consequences are for sheep, not farmers. A citizen cannot be caught speeding without consequences – but you are above all that now, no matter what hells you unleash on the world.

People want political power because they want something for nothing, and they want to escape the consequences of their evil actions – we want to assure you that you have now *fully* achieved these goals. You will never have to worry about losing your house, your job, your money, your freedom – and with this kind of immunity from political, legal and economic reality, you can project all the serene confidence of a sea captain being helicoptered to safety while his ship slowly sinks.

We can also guarantee you that you will never face *any* tough questions from the media. Anyone who gets to interview you will be so thrilled at the opportunity, and so excited to be advancing his career, that he will only lob you softball setups. It's true that a single question might be asked, such as, "do you think that X was a mistake?" but we can assure you with perfect equanimity that whatever you answer will be accepted, and no follow-up questions will be asked. You will always have the final say, and if anyone does dare to ask you a follow-up question, all you have to do is act mildly irritated, and insist that you have already answered that question.

If anyone persists, not to worry, his career will be over, because about 10,000 empty-headed pundits will take to the airwaves claiming to be shocked and appalled at the way that you were browbeaten and harangued, and demanding to know what your problem is, and who you think you are, and so on.

We know, we know – it sounds impossible, but it's a guaranteed fix, every single time. It's as predictable as hungry dogs chasing a dead rabbit on a string.

ETHICS

There are two kinds of ethics that you need to be aware of – it is very likely that you are already aware of them, since you are where you are, but it's worth going over them one more time.

When slaves evaluate masters, relativism and deference and working together and respecting differences of opinion are key.

When masters evaluate other masters, bipartisanship and putting aside differences and working together and respecting differences of opinion are also key.

This falls into the old category of "turn the other cheek."

When masters evaluate *slaves*, however, it's total "eye for an eye" time!

For instance, if you propose health care legislation that will force people to do stuff, it's very important that you respect the other parties' right to disagree with your proposal. However, once it becomes law, no mere *citizen* is ever allowed to act on his or her disagreement with *you*!

Debates are for the masters, enforcement is for the slaves.

You are allowed to debate whether or not to go to war, citizens are not allowed to choose whether or not they fund the war, or are drafted to get killed in it. You are allowed to debate whether to subsidize some group, citizens are never allowed to choose whether *they* subsidize that group.

Free will is for the masters – slaves get the determinism of their masters' whims.

In case you have any concern that someone will point out the ridiculousness of all this, do not fear! The moment that anyone argues that we don't need violent masters – that such masters are in fact hellishly destructive – all the slaves in the *world* will gang up on such an exposed truth-teller, saying, in effect, "We are not slaves if you don't point out our masters!"

This reaction is all based on propaganda that is carefully layered in throughout government education – and all education is government education, because we regulate and control private schools and universities as well.

The propaganda is, like all propaganda, completely insane, but through calm repetition and attacking dissenters, it quickly gets accepted as an obvious truth.

The propaganda is this:

1. *The government provides service X.*
2. *If the government does not provide service X, service X will never be provided.*
3. *Therefore, anyone arguing against the government providing service X is arguing against the necessity or value of service X.*

It seems almost embarrassing to point out the foolishness of these arguments, but in the highly unlikely event you ever get a question on this, it's good to have an "answer."

According to the democratic model, governments only do what the majority of citizens want them to do. "The will of the majority," is one of our central gods, which cannot speak for itself, of course, and therefore kindly allows us to, um, speak for it.

Democratic governments only help the poor, then, because *the majority of citizens want them to.* If governments reflect the will of the people, then whatever governments do is entirely unnecessary, because the majority want to do it anyway.

The more that people get attacked for not caring about the poor, the less the government needs to do anything about the poor, because *the attacks reflect a general preference to help the poor.* The only practical argument for the continuance of a government program would be if everybody had a strong desire to get rid of it, because then, it could be argued, they did not care about its recipients. If someone said, "Let's get rid of the welfare state," and everyone cheered and joined in, we might very well have some concern about the fate of the poor – the fact that everyone *defends* the welfare state means that the poor will be perfectly well taken care of in a free society.

Ah, the weariness of these ridiculous arguments! We do sometimes wish that people would become just a little bit smarter, so we could all eventually become free, but we are as trapped by the livestock's illusions as they are.

Exploitation

There are two classes of parasites on the productive classes – the poor and the political. In the old days, Marxists used to blather on about the exploitation of the poor by capitalists, which was utter nonsense. When the capitalists were "exploiting" the workers in the mid 19th century, their real wages *doubled* – we democratic masters have had our real claws on them for the past 40 years, and real wages have not only stagnated and fallen, but educational standards have collapsed, incarceration rates have skyrocketed, living conditions have deteriorated – and the remaining social services we provide (bribes) are all going to collapse because we have sold everyone off piecemeal under the guise of "national debt" (because the real term – *serfdom* – is just too accurate to be accepted).

The old-style capitalists "exploited" the poor by paying them ever-higher wages – we exploit them by selling both them and their kids off to whoever will shove a thin dime in our direction – dropping a penny in the hollow plates of the poor, keeping eight cents for ourselves, and using the last penny as collateral to borrow ten more.

But the merchant class is very useful to us, in more ways than as tax cattle, tax collectors, and productive livestock – they also shield us from popular anger at the inevitable results of our predations. When we pay ourselves with the monopoly money (literally) of their futures, prices go up. Who does the public get angry at? Us? Ha ha, get real, we don't teach them a damn thing about *real* economics – no, they get angry at the checkout girl at the local convenience store for high prices – and of course we always promise to "investigate" the source of such shocking inflation. It's pretty easy to pretend to investigate a mirror.

The strange thing as well is that we educate their kids, and then they expect these lost souls to be somehow objective about us! Imagine if a kid went to a school run by a government Post Office – would you expect him to learn any form of critical thinking about the Post Office? Of course not – he would get endless lessons on how wonderful, benevolent and friendly Post Office workers were, and how before the Post Office became a government monopoly, private mail carriers stole checks from starving widows, abused their workers and overcharged their helpless customers. You wouldn't expect even a sliver of truth to fall through the cracks of propaganda, but all this – and more, since the Post Office can't start wars – is inflicted on the helpless kids held prisoner in state "schools." So people arrive at adulthood worshipping the State that stole from their parents, crushed their minds under forced indoctrination, sold them into serfdom for the rest of their lives, and programmed them for endless obedience.

Imagine if we said that Goldman Sachs should run all the government schools – just picture the howls of indignation that would arise, shrill shrieks of the dangers of bias, indoctrination and programming! Ah, but give the children to the State, and everyone smiles benignly, certain that objectivity, reason and a well-tempered love of children and learning will reign supreme.

Ahhh, it does turn the stomach so at times! Everyone knows that teachers don't give even *half* a rat's ass about the kids – and the test is so pitifully easy that everyone knows what it is. Just remind the teachers that kids don't benefit from having over two months off in the summer – and it's hell for parents as well of course – and cite the statistics about how well kids do when they're in school year round, and don't forget everything over the summer. How will the teachers react? Meh, to ask the question is to answer it.

CHILDHOOD <> PERSONHOOD

The key to tyranny is to treat kids as somewhere between pets and hobos. If a child never thinks of himself as a full person, he will never aspire to be more than a "citizen" – i.e. to be owned, and sold, and ordered around. (People take pride in being 'citizens,' which is completely mad, since 'citizenship' means that they have been granted the 'right' to work, travel and live, which are all supposed to be 'inalienable' anyway...)

For example - imagine, as Murray Rothbard once wrote, that the government should take over magazines and books, and limit readership by local geography, and hire, fire and control all writers, editors and reporters, and force people to pay for them even if they never read them – what an unholy outcry would arise! Cries of 'censorship' and 'tyranny' would echo in tinny indignation from bosom to heaving bosom! Ah, but inflict far *worse* controls on children – force them into local schools, control all the teachers and curriculum (even for 'private' schools) and not only are the voices of protest silent, but are only raised *against* anyone who dares to suggest that the free minds of helpless children are far more important than the recreational reading tastes of adults...

You'll get a kick out of this one too – ok – use government power to force everyone to pay for the indoctrination of children, force the kids to sit in dusty, still rows, barely allowed to blink – and then drug the living crap out of them if they get bored and restless – and keep them trapped there, year after year – and then tell them that their masters won the war that set them free, against National Socialism and communism! Can you imagine telling children in an entirely communist environment – public schools – that communism is the enemy? Of course, they'll just write it down and regurgitate it whenever you want, because they're terrified of being drugged – and then you have to tell them, of course, that communist dictatorships used the lie called "mental illness" to drug anyone who didn't fit in and obey the rulers!

Freedom is for the adults – communism is for the children.

Science

We have a complicated relationship with science – we need it, for weapons and tax livestock management (imagine how hard it would be to collect taxes without computers) – so we need science to flourish, but we also need to control it. The way we do this is to continually program the population to view science as a productive but dangerous force that will destroy the world if not tightly controlled. This is utterly absurd, of course, since it was our control of science through the Manhattan Project that created weapons that actually *could* destroy the world, but then we just tell the sheeple that, yanno, worse things would have happened if we didn't make nukes, and they all baa and agree and eat the leftover grass we shovel into their troughs.

So we do this sort of "Sorcerer's Apprentice" thing, where science is great to begin with, but then grows and grows and gets out of control and needs to be shut down in an extremity of CGI adventure. Naturally, we're *really* talking about ourselves, the government itself, but no one wants to think about that, so they imagine that it's all about robots and computers and carbon footprints and machines that make hot dogs in the sky…

People will always choose a thousand fairy tales over one basic fact.

Except us, perhaps. Our understanding of – and immunity to – sentimentality is our greatest power. We are the lions who hunt with sentimental pictures of little kittens.

FROM HERE...

At this point, it does pain me to tell you that you will soon have the rather unenviable task of informing the livestock that they are pretty much screwed.

There is no way in god's green earth that our system will last even another few years, which means that you will have dust off and start playing the good old 'sacrifice violin.'

Now this traditional instrument may sound screechy and ridiculous to your ears but trust us, just keep playing and everyone will dance in a line for you.

Just tell them that biiiig hardships are coming, that we as a nation are being 'tested,' and that we all need to 'pull together' and shoulder our common burdens, and look out for the most vulnerable among us, and that to achieve a new dawn, sacrifices need to be made, and hint strongly that bad forces outside your control – or before your time – have robbed the people, and will be held accountable, but that we all need to look to the future, and remember that we as a people can do anything we set our minds and wills to, and we defeated the prior tyrannies etc etc etc.

For some reason, people always take a dark masochistic delight in struggling through trying times where they all have to "pull together" and "make sacrifices" and strive to achieve the best in tragic times and so on. Probably boredom and self-contempt for their own hypocrisy, but who knows, and who cares? The important thing is that government schools and all the endless lies about past wars and depressions – that the best in people comes out in the worst of times and so on – have all programmed citizens to react with dark and lascivious glee when we demand that they spend a generation eating shit for our mistakes.

Of course, people love to punish themselves for their own hypocrisies and various other sins, and Lord knows the average state-sucking slut voter has more than enough to feel guilty about, trying to wheedle something for nothing out of the government, the future, their own *children* for heaven's sake! So when sacrifice is called for, most people feel secretly relieved, since all these trials, tribulations and common burdens effectively squelch any substantial social, economic or political criticisms.

"Pull together" unleashes the most savage social censorship imaginable. During the coming time of crisis, if the young people justly point fingers at the greed and hypocrisy of their elders, they will be sternly told that we all have to *pull together*, and there's no point playing the "blame game" now. If the young point out that *they* were never allowed such a mealy-mouthed avoidance strategy when they were growing up, they will be told that they are quibbling and refusing to let go of the past and so on. Ha ha, imagine a teenager trying those strategies about failing to take out the garbage, and you will instantly see how much these cowardly redirects stink!

So — self-flagellation for past crimes and avoidance of just accusations from past victims — these motives will trigger such hellish attacks on freethinkers that only the truly crazed will continue to raise these issues… (If you want to know more about this phenomenon, just remember how few Europeans criticized the ruling classes for two World Wars in two generations, but rather took pride in 'winning' a bloodbath that cost over 50 million lives — and contrast that with how they treat a waiter who forgets their *food order*.)

So the plan is always the same — we pillage, plunder and bribe — then demand sacrifices from our victims. To get the general idea, picture a rapist demanding a drive home from his victim.

Anyone who does not play along with this insanity will just be branded a malcontent, not a "team player" — and mocked and ostracized. Fortunately, we have bred our livestock to be so dependent on social approval that most everyone will find this unbearable, and slink back into the single file line to the graveyard, pushing their bewildered and resentful children ahead of them...

Conclusion

So remember – you're going to be taken care of, that's the first thing to really understand. You can't go broke, you can't go hungry, you can't lose your house, you can't really be fired, and people will pay hundreds of thousands of dollars to hear you speak every day for the rest of your life. You will get libraries named after you, receive multimillion dollar book deals, and a guaranteed gold-plated pension with free health care for the rest of your life.

You have absolutely nothing to worry about. You have the softest seat on the biggest lifeboat.

This is, to a large degree, the source of your weird confidence, which separates you from the herd, and which they imagine is why you are their leader.

The reality is that they have endless worries that you don't have, and so you can just join us, floating above the petty fears of the masses, serene and secure like the ancient gods we have always been.

So go out among the crowds and make pretty noises with your velvet throat. Distract these fools with your eloquence while we finish pillaging their pockets. Empty out the remainder of your soul driving the sheeple off a cliff – it may haunt the remnants of your integrity, but don't worry: we do still have that stamp just waiting for your smiling face.